MILESTONES AND MOMENTS

MILESTONES AND MOMENTS

A GUIDE TO YOUR BABY'S FIRST YEAR

By Pearlyn Henry-Burrell

Milestones and Moments: A Guide To Your Baby's First Year.

Compiled by Pearlyn Henry-Burrell.

Publishing assistance by:

The Self-Publish Connection
Kingston, Jamaica
https://theselfpublishconnection.com
IG: @theselfpublishconnection
Facebook: The Self-Publish Connection
YouTube: @theselfpublishconnection

ISBN: 978-1-0369-0755-6

Contents

Preface

Welcome to *Milestones and Moments: A Guide to Your Baby's First Year*. As a new or returning parent, you embark on an incredible journey filled with love, joy, and countless unforgettable moments. This book is designed to support you as you navigate the exciting and sometimes overwhelming terrain of early childhood. This book is part of your support system.

Throughout the first year of your baby's life, you will witness remarkable growth and development across all domains (language, physical, cognitive, social, and emotional). From their first smile and coo to their first steps and words, each milestone is a precious memory to cherish. This book will provide valuable information and guidance to help you understand and appreciate these special moments. Enjoy every moment as it unfolds.

We have carefully curated content to cover various topics, including communication and language, physical development, cognitive skills, social and emotional growth, and common concerns. Whether you seek practical advice or emotional support or want to celebrate your baby's achievements, this book is here to assist you. Your learning partner in the journey of parenthood.

Remember, every child is unique, and their development may vary. The information in this book is intended as a general guide and should not replace professional advice from your paediatrician. Seek professional support and guidance as the journey unfolds.

We hope *Milestones and Moments* will be helpful as you cherish the precious memories of your baby's first year.

Enjoy the journey!

Dedicated to All Caesarean Section Mothers

To all mothers who have experienced the strength and resilience of a Caesarean section, especially to single mothers, this is for you. May this dedication be a tribute to your courage and the incredible journey you've embarked on. Remember, your strength and love are a testament to your unwavering bond with your child.

You are getting stronger every day!

Developmental Milestones: A Guide for Parents

Developmental milestones are age-related abilities that most children achieve. Tracking these milestones can help you understand your baby's development and identify potential delays.

Key Developmental Milestones:

- **Physical Development:** Rolling over, sitting up, crawling, standing, and walking.
- **Cognitive Development:** Responding to sounds, recognising faces, object permanence, and problem-solving.
- **Language Development:** Cooing, babbling, first words, understanding simple words and phrases.
- **Social and Emotional Development:** Smiling, laughing, showing emotions, forming attachments.

Tracking Your Baby's Progress:

- **Regular Check-ups:** Schedule regular check-ups with your paediatrician to monitor your baby's development.
- **Developmental Checklists:** Use developmental checklists or apps to track milestones.
- **Observe Your Baby:** Pay attention to your baby's behaviour and interactions.
- **Trust Your Instincts:** Don't hesitate to talk to your paediatrician if you have concerns.

Delayed Development: When to Seek Help

If your baby is significantly behind in their development, it's important to consult with your paediatrician. Early intervention can make a big difference.

Signs of Delayed Development:

- Not meeting milestones by the expected age.
- Significant delays in language development.
- Poor motor skills.
- Lack of social interaction.
- Unusual behaviours.

Chapter 1: Milestones for the First Few Months

Physical Development

- **Tracking Your Baby's Growth:** You must regularly **monitor** your baby's weight, length, and head circumference to ensure healthy growth.
- **Head Control:** Take time to observe your baby's ability to steadily hold their head up when supported.
- **Rolling Over:** Attempting to roll over is a significant milestone! Watch for your baby's first rolling-over attempts, usually from tummy to back or vice versa.
- **Sitting Up:** We cannot wait to see when your little one begins to sit! Support your baby's back and help them practice sitting up with your hands.

Cognitive Development

- **Object Permanence:** This is a test to see if your little one understands that things continue to exist even when out of sight. Test your baby's understanding of object permanence by hiding a toy and seeing if they search for it.
- **Cause-and-Effect:** Response to cause and effect is a good measure of your child's awareness and response to stimulus. Observe your baby's reactions to simple cause-and-effect actions, such as shaking a rattle or banging a toy.
- **Attention Span: Babies have very short attention spans.** Notice how long your baby can focus on a particular object or activity.

Social and Emotional Development

- **Smiling:** Oh, that smile! Watch for your baby's first smiles, which are often reflexive but later become more social.
- **Cooing:** Babies talk too! Listen to your baby's early vocalisations, such as cooing and babbling. This is a good time for serve and return conversations. Talk with and to your babies.
- **Attachment Formation:** Young children thrive in warm and responsive relationships. Observe your baby's developing attachment to you and other primary caregivers. Secured attachment is very important to healthy emotional development.
- **Social Interaction:** These are magic moments! Encourage social interaction by talking to your baby, playing games, and introducing them to others.

Communication and Language

Babies communicate their needs and emotions through a variety of nonverbal cues, such as:

- **Crying:** This is how babies tell us they have arrived safely in a new and exciting world! Crying is the most obvious way babies express their needs, whether hunger, discomfort or simply a desire for attention.
- **Cooing:** This is how babies talk! This is a series of soft, vowel-like sounds babies begin making around two (2) months old. It's a way for them to practice their vocal cords and explore different sounds.

- **Babbling:** As babies age, they combine consonants and vowels into babbling sounds like "mamama" or "dadada." This is a crucial step in language development.
- **Facial expressions:** Babies have emotions too! Babies can express many emotions through facial expressions, from happiness to sadness to surprise.

Gestures: Pay keen attention to that pointing finger! Babies may use gestures like pointing or waving to communicate their wants and needs.

Key Activities to Foster Development in The First Few Months

Physical Development

- **Tummy Time: This is a special time between you and your baby.** Encourage your baby to spend time on their tummy to strengthen their neck, back, and shoulder muscles. Provide lots of opportunities for tummy time.
- **Floor Play:** Get down on the floor with your baby. Provide a safe, clean space for your baby to explore and play on the floor.
- **Sensory Play:** Get creative and stimulate your baby's senses by touching different textures, playing with water, and listening to various sounds.
- **Baby Massage:** Babies need massages too! Gently massage your baby's body to promote relaxation and muscle development.

Cognitive Development

- **Object Permanence Activities:** Play hide-and-seek games, peek-a-boo, or use object permanence boxes to help your baby understand that objects continue to exist even when out of sight.
- **Cause-and-Effect Toys:** You should provide toys to encourage your baby to explore cause-and-effect relationships, such as stacking blocks, squeezing toys, or pushing buttons.
- **Language Development:** Spend lots of time talking to your baby, reading books aloud, and singing songs to stimulate their language development. Ask lots of questions and listen for their age-appropriate responses!

Social and Emotional Development

- **Face-to-Face Interaction:** The eyes are the gateways to the brain. Spend quality time looking into your baby's eyes and engaging in face-to-face interactions.
- **Social Play:** Most skills your baby will learn will come from social interactions. Encourage social play by introducing your baby to other children and adults. Join playgroups in your local community.
- **Emotional Expression:** Verbal tagging of emotions by adults is very important as it can help young children to name their emotions. Help your baby express their emotions by labelling their feelings and providing comfort and support. They do not have the words to express their feelings at this stage.
- **Mirror Play:** Let your child see the beauty of their face! Use a mirror to help your baby explore their reflection and develop self-awareness. The face has some fascinating features!

Communication and Language

Parents and caregivers can be vital in supporting a baby's language development. Here are some tips:

- **Talk to your baby often:** Talk, talk and more talk! Even if your baby can't understand your words, talking to them helps them become familiar with language sounds.
- **Read to your baby:** Make reading to your baby a daily routine. Reading aloud exposes babies to a variety of words and sounds. Show them those pictures, too!
- **Sing songs and nursery rhymes:** Let your melodious voice fill the atmosphere! Singing is a fun way to help babies develop their language skills and bond with you. Nursery rhymes open the door for lots of sound awareness and prime the pump for further early literacy skills
- **Respond to your baby's cues:** Listen and respond to your baby's cues. When your baby cries or makes other sounds, respond promptly to tell them you're listening.
- **Limit screen time:** Excessive screen time can hinder language development and limit quality bonding time with a primary caregiver. Children under 2 years old should not have access to screen time. This time is about forming lasting relationships with their caregivers. Those serve and return and bonding moments matter!

Mindful Munchies: A Foundation for Life

The first few months of a child's life are a period of rapid growth and development, laying the groundwork for their future. During this crucial time, nurturing your baby's physical, emotional, and cognitive needs is paramount. Providing a loving, stimulating environment, responding to their cues, and engaging in interactive play will foster their development and create a strong bond between you and your child. These early experiences will have a lasting impact on their lifelong learning and well-being.

Chapter 2: Milestones for 3-6 Months

Physical Development

- **Crawling:** Be watchful! Watch for your baby's first attempts at crawling, which may involve scooting, rolling, or crawling on their hands and knees.
- **Teething:** This is a significant milestone to celebrate! Prepare for your baby's first teeth to emerge and provide relief with teething rings or cool objects. This can be a bit challenging for your baby.
- **Reaching and Grasping:** Encourage your baby to reach for and grasp objects with their hands.
- **Sitting with Support:** Help your baby practice sitting up with support from your hands or a pillow. Be careful. This should not be a forced process.

Cognitive Development

- **Curiosity:** Young children are naturally curious! Observe your baby's growing curiosity as they explore their surroundings and investigate new objects. Give your child lots of opportunities to extend their curiosity.
- **Problem-Solving:** Give them things to figure out! Watch for your baby's developing problem-solving skills, such as figuring out how to reach a toy or open a container. They will enjoy every moment.
- **Object Permanence:** Test your baby's understanding of object permanence by hiding a toy and seeing if they search for it.

Social and Emotional Development

- **Babbling:** Spend time listening to your baby's babbling and encouraging them to make sounds by imitating them.
- **Developing Preferences:** Give your baby choices! Notice your baby's preferences for certain toys, foods, or activities.
- **Social Interactions:** Observe your baby's growing interest in interacting with others, such as smiling, laughing, and waving. Keep your baby engaged in activities that can build their social and emotional well-being.
- **Stranger Anxiety:** Be aware of your baby's developing stranger anxiety and provide comfort and reassurance. Never force your child to go to anyone toward whom they are showing social anxiety. You must respect your child's preferences and safeguard your child against harm.

Communication and Language

- **Babbling:** Babbling continues at this stage. Join in and encourage your baby to babble by imitating their sounds and using a variety of vocalisations.
- **Understanding Simple Words:** Communication is about speaking as it is about listening and comprehending. Observe if your baby understands simple words and phrases like "no" or "bye-bye."
- **Responding to Sounds:** Look to see if your baby's auditory skills are developing right! Notice how your baby responds to different sounds, such as clapping or a doorbell.
- **Early Signs of Language:** Remember that non-verbal communication is important to your baby's development. Look for early signs of language development, such as pointing to objects or using gestures to communicate.

Key Activities to Foster Development in 3-6 Months

Physical Development

- **Tummy Time:** Encourage tummy time to strengthen your baby's upper body and prepare for crawling.
- **Floor Play:** Your baby still needs lots of floor play. Provide a safe space for your baby to explore and play on the floor.
- **Reaching and Grasping:** Begin working on your baby's motor development. Offer a variety of objects for your baby to reach for and grasp, such as soft toys, rattles, or blocks.
- **Sitting with Support:** Remember, this should never be about hastening your baby's development. The focus should be on supporting or facilitating development. Do this by helping your baby practice sitting up with support from your hands or a pillow.

Cognitive Development

- **Object Permanence Activities:** Play hide-and-seek and object permanence games to reinforce this concept.
- **Cause-and-Effect Toys:** Offer toys encouraging your baby to explore cause-and-effect relationships, such as stacking blocks, squeezing toys, or pushing buttons.
- **Shape Sorters:** Introduce shape sorters to help your baby develop fine motor skills and spatial reasoning.

Social and Emotional Development

- **Social Interactions:** Encourage your baby to interact with other children and adults, such as playing peek-a-boo or clapping hands together.

- **Emotional Expression:** Label your baby's emotions to help them understand and express their feelings. This will be important later in life, so support their emotional literacy as they develop an awareness of their emotions.
- **Mirror Play:** Use a mirror to help your baby explore their reflection and develop self-awareness.

Communication and Language

- **Babbling and Imitating Sounds:** Continue to imitate your baby's babbling and encourage them to make new sounds.
- **Simple Commands:** Use simple commands, such as "wave bye-bye" or "come here," to help your baby understand and respond to language.
- **Reading Aloud:** Read books to your baby to introduce them to language, stories, and pictures.
- **Singing Songs:** Sing songs and nursery rhymes to help your baby develop a sense of rhythm and language.

Mindful Munches: Nurturing the Growing Mind

Remember that the 3-6-month period is a time of rapid cognitive development. Your baby is now exploring their world with newfound curiosity, learning about objects, sounds, and people. You can support their intellectual growth by providing a stimulating environment filled with toys, books, and opportunities for exploration. Engaging in interactive play, responding to their babbling, and introducing new words will help them develop their language skills and lay the foundation for future learning. Remember, every moment spent nurturing your baby's mind is an investment in their future!

Chapter 3: Milestones for 6-9 Months

Physical Development

- **Sitting with Support:** Your child may be ready to sit up with less support at this stage. Help your baby practice sitting up with minimal support from your hands or a pillow.
- **Pulling to Stand:** Your courageous child may attempt to pull themselves up to stand! Encourage your baby to pull themselves up to a standing position by holding onto furniture. Be the watchful eyes and the stretching hands ready to catch them!
- **Cruising:** Observe your baby's first attempts at cruising, which involves walking sideways while holding onto furniture.
- **Fine Motor Skills:** Motor development is important. It gives lots of opportunities for large and fine motor development. Practice activities that help develop your baby's fine motor skills, such as pinching small objects or stacking blocks.

Cognitive Development

- **Increased Understanding of Language:** They are getting smarter every day! Notice how your baby responds to simple commands and understands more words.
- **Object Permanence:** Continue to test your baby's understanding of object permanence by hiding a toy and seeing if they search for it in multiple locations. This is amazing to watch!
- **Cause-and-Effect Relationships:** Your baby is a young explorer! Observe your baby's ability to understand cause-

and-effect relationships, such as pushing a toy car to make it move.

Social and Emotional Development

- **Developing Emotions:** Recognize your baby's developing emotions, such as fear, anger, and jealousy. Remember that you need to observe to understand your child's emotional language. It is also important to set expectations and boundaries. Teach expected behaviours.
- **Social Interactions:** Be part of friendship or parent groups in your local community. Encourage your baby to play with other children and interact with adults.
- **Separation Anxiety:** Be aware of your baby's developing separation anxiety and provide comfort and reassurance. Do not force or scold your child for showing separation anxiety. Be gentle and reassuring.

Communication and Language

- **Babbling and Imitating Sounds:** Encourage your baby to babble and imitate sounds.
- **Understanding Simple Words:** Provide a language-rich environment for your baby to thrive in. Observe if your baby understands more words and can follow simple commands.
- **Using Gestures:** Notice if your baby uses gestures, such as pointing or waving, to communicate. Add words to the baby's gestures. Remember, at this age, you are their interpreter!
- **Early Signs of Language:** Look for early signs of language development, such as using single words or combining sounds. Praise and expand their vocabulary by exposing them to various oral models.

Key Activities to Foster Development in 6-9 Months

Physical Development

- **Encourage Crawling:** Provide opportunities for your baby to practice crawling, such as placing toys out of reach or creating obstacle courses. Enjoy these moments!
- **Pull-Up Bar:** Install a pull-up bar at a safe height to encourage your baby to pull themselves up and practice standing.
- **Walking with Support:** Hold your baby's hands and help them practice walking while providing support.
- **Fine Motor Skills:** Offer a variety of toys and objects that encourage your baby to develop fine motor skills, such as stacking blocks, turning doorknobs, or playing with small toys.

Cognitive Development

- **Object Permanence Games:** Play hide-and-seek and object permanence games to reinforce this concept.
- **Shape Sorters:** Introduce more challenging shape sorters with smaller shapes and more compartments.
- **Problem-Solving Activities:** Provide opportunities for your baby to solve simple problems, such as opening containers or figuring out how to fit objects into shapes.
- **Cause-and-Effect Toys:** Offer toys encouraging your baby to explore cause-and-effect relationships, such as pushing buttons to activate sounds or lights.

Social and Emotional Development

- **Social Interactions:** Encourage your baby to play with other children and interact with adults.

- **Emotional Expression:** Label your baby's emotions and help them understand and express their feelings.
- **Separation Anxiety:** Help your baby cope with separation anxiety by providing comfort and reassurance when you leave.
- **Independence:** Encourage your baby's developing independence by allowing them to explore their surroundings safely.

Communication and Language

- **Babbling and Imitating Sounds:** Encourage your baby to babble and imitate sounds.
- **Simple Commands:** Use simple commands and gestures to help your baby understand and follow instructions.
- **Sign Language:** Teach your baby simple sign language gestures to help them communicate their needs and wants.

Reading Aloud: Continue to read books to your baby to introduce them to language, stories, and pictures.

Mindful Munches: Nurturing the Magic of Early Development

Remember that the 6-9 months is a magical time for your baby's development. Their brains are growing rapidly, absorbing information and learning new skills daily. During this time, providing a stimulating environment, engaging in interactive play, and encouraging communication will foster their cognitive, social, and emotional growth. These early experiences will shape your child's future development and lay the foundation for a lifelong love of learning.

Let these early moments count!

Chapter 4: Milestones for 9-12 Months

Physical Development

- **Crawling Confidently:** Your baby is now on the move! Observe your baby's improved crawling skills and speed. Make sure that your environment is safe and free from things that can cause harm to your baby. Electrical plugs must be covered, all water containers covered, and harmful substances must be stored outside your child's reach.
- **Standing Independently:** Be the gentle guide during these moments. Encourage your baby to practice standing independently, holding furniture or a walker.
- **Taking First Steps:** You have been waiting long for this magical moment! Celebrate your baby's first steps, which may occur between 9 and 12 months.
- **Fine Motor Skills:** Continue to practice activities that develop your baby's fine motor skills, such as pinching small objects, turning doorknobs, or using utensils. It also gives opportunities for large muscle development.

Cognitive Development

- **Language Development:** Listen to your baby's developing language skills, including using single words and simple phrases. Remember to support this process by having many intentional conversations with your baby.
- **Problem-Solving Abilities:** Observe your baby's ability to solve more complex problems, such as opening containers or fitting shapes into corresponding holes

- **Object Permanence:** Test your baby's understanding of object permanence by hiding a toy and seeing if they search for it in multiple locations.

Social and Emotional Development

- **Developing Independence:** Notice your baby's growing desire for independence, such as wanting to do things independently. Give them age-appropriate autonomy within limits.
- **Separation Anxiety:** Be aware of your baby's separation anxiety and provide comfort and reassurance when you leave.
- **Social Interactions:** Encourage your baby to play with other children and interact with adults.
- **Developing Emotions:** Recognize your baby's expanding emotions, including frustration, jealousy, and empathy.

Communication and Language

- **Using Single Words:** Language development is rapid during the first few years of your child's life. Listen for your baby's first single words, such as "mama," "dada," or "ball."
- **Combining Sounds:** They are getting better with time! Observe your baby's attempts to combine sounds, such as "mamma" or "dada."
- **Understanding Simple Instructions:** Test your baby's understanding of simple instructions, such as "Come here" or "Give me the toy."
- **Using Gestures:** Encourage your baby to use gestures to communicate their needs and wants.

Key Activities to Foster Development in 9-12 Months

Physical Development

- **Encourage Walking:** Your job is to provide opportunities for your baby to practice walking, such as holding their hands or using a walker.
- **Climbing and Exploring:** Build on your child's natural curiosity. Allow your baby to safely explore their surroundings, including climbing stairs or onto furniture.
- **Fine Motor Skills:** Continue to practice activities that develop fine motor skills, such as using utensils, turning pages in a book, or stacking blocks. Also, include activities to strengthen your baby's large muscle development.

Cognitive Development

- **Problem-Solving Activities:** Provide opportunities for your baby to solve more complex problems, such as opening containers or fitting shapes into corresponding holes.
- **Sorting Activities:** Introduce sporting activities, such as sorting objects by colour, shape, or size.
- **Counting and Numbers:** Start introducing basic counting concepts and numbers.
- **Memory Games:** Play simple memory games with your baby to help them develop their memory skills.

Social and Emotional Development

- **Social Interactions:** Encourage your baby to play with other children and interact with adults.
- **Emotional Expression:** Label your baby's emotions and help them understand and express their feelings.

- **Independence:** Encourage your baby's developing independence by allowing them to dress or feed themselves. Let them take charge in a safe and age-appropriate way!
- **Sharing and Taking Turns:** Teach your baby the importance of sharing and taking turns with toys and activities. Turn-taking is an essential skill.

Communication and Language

- **Expanding Vocabulary:** Introduce new words and encourage your baby to use them in sentences.
- **Following Simple Instructions:** Test your baby's understanding of simple instructions and respond to your requests. Do they demonstrate age-appropriate understanding?
- **Encouraging Speech:** Talk to your baby frequently, read books aloud, and sing songs to stimulate their language development.
- **Signing:** Consider teaching your baby basic sign language gestures to help them communicate their needs and wants.

Mindful Munches: Nurturing the Foundations of Learning

Remember that the 9-12-month period is a remarkable time of rapid growth and development for your baby. During these months, their brains develop astonishingly, laying the foundation for future learning and cognitive abilities. Providing a stimulating environment filled with opportunities for exploration, communication, and social interaction is crucial. Encourage your baby's curiosity, respond to their needs, and celebrate milestones. By nurturing their natural desire to learn and grow, you invest in a bright future filled with endless possibilities.

Get excited about how far you and your baby have come!

Chapter 5: Celebrating Milestones Birth -12 Months

Tracking Your Baby's Progress

- **Developmental Charts:** Use age-appropriate developmental charts or checklists to track your baby's progress in various areas, such as physical development, cognitive skills, and social and emotional development. All domains are interrelated, with one impacting the other.
- **Comparing to Norms:** Understand that developmental charts provide general guidelines and that individual variations are common. Your child is unique.
- **Consulting with Your Paediatrician:** Discuss your baby's development with your paediatrician to address any concerns or questions. Do not make assumptions about your baby.

Celebrating Achievements

- **Recognising Milestones:** Celebrate your baby's milestones, such as their first steps, words, or birthday. Get a journal to document your interpretation of the journey! You are growing and changing, too!
- **Creating Memories:** Take pictures and videos to capture these special moments and create lasting memories. You would be amazed at how many wonderful moments that you have shared!
- **Expressing Love and Support:** Show your love and support for your baby's achievements, no matter how small they may seem.

Understanding Individual Differences

- **Every Baby is Unique:** Recognise that every baby develops at their own pace and has unique strengths and weaknesses.
- **Avoiding Comparisons:** Refrain from comparing your baby to other children, as this can lead to unnecessary stress and anxiety. Each baby is unique.

Seeking Professional Advice: If you have concerns about your baby's development, consult your paediatrician or a child development specialist. Seeking professional help is the first step in the right direction.

Mindful Munches: A Joyful Journey

As your baby reaches new milestones, take time to celebrate their achievements. Whether it's their first steps, word, or any other significant accomplishment, these moments are precious and should be cherished. Acknowledge their efforts with praise, encouragement, and love. Celebrating milestones reinforces your baby's confidence, strengthens your bond, and creates lasting memories.

Chapter 6: Supporting Your Baby's Development

Creating a Stimulating Environment

- **Safe and Secure Space:** Provide a safe and secure environment for your baby to explore and learn.
- **Variety of Experiences:** Offer various experiences, such as different sounds, textures, sights, and smells.
- **Age-Appropriate Toys:** Provide toys appropriate for your baby's age and developmental level.
- **Natural Light and Outdoor Time:** Expose your baby to natural light and outdoor activities whenever possible.

Engaging in Play Activities

- **Floor Play:** Encourage floor play to promote physical development and exploration.
- **Sensory Play:** Provide opportunities for sensory play, such as playing with water, sand, or sensory bins.
- **Interactive Toys:** Offer toys that encourage interaction, such as cause-and-effect or those that require problem-solving skills.
- **Imitation Games:** Play games that involve imitation, such as copying sounds or actions.

Reading and Storytelling

- **Early Exposure:** Start reading to your baby from a young age before they can understand the words.
- **Choosing Appropriate Books:** Select books with colourful illustrations and simple, age-appropriate stories.

- **Engaging with the Story:** Use different voices and expressions to make reading more enjoyable for your baby.
- **Discussing the Story:** Ask your baby questions about the story and encourage them to interact.

Mindful Munches: Supporting Your Baby's Holistic Development

Providing a nurturing and stimulating environment is essential for your baby's development. Engage in interactive play, respond to their cues, and encourage exploration. Read to them, sing songs, and expose them to various experiences. By nurturing their natural curiosity and providing growth opportunities, you're helping your baby reach their full potential.

Chapter 7: Common Concerns and Questions

Delayed Milestones

- **Recognising Delays:** Be aware of potential delays in your baby's development, such as not meeting key milestones within expected timeframes.
- **Consulting with Your Paediatrician:** Discuss your concerns with your paediatrician, who can assess your baby's development and provide guidance.
- **Seeking Additional Support:** Consider seeking additional support from developmental specialists or therapists if necessary.

Early Signs of Autism

- **Understanding Autism:** Learn about the early signs of autism, such as delayed language development, difficulty with social interaction, and repetitive behaviours.
- **Seeking Early Intervention:** If you notice any early signs of autism, consult with your paediatrician or a developmental specialist for early intervention services.
- **Resources and Support:** Connect with organisations and support groups for families of children with autism.

Feeding and Nutrition

- **Breastfeeding vs. formula:** Many parents wonder whether to breastfeed or use formula. Both options have benefits, and your best choice depends on your circumstances.

Breastfeeding vs. Formula: A Personalised Choice

The decision to breastfeed or formula-feed is deeply personal, and there's no right or wrong answer. Both options offer unique advantages; your best choice will depend on your circumstances and priorities.

Benefits of Breastfeeding

- **Nutritional Benefits:** Breast milk is specifically designed to meet a baby's nutritional needs, providing essential antibodies and nutrients.
- **Reduced Risk of Illness:** Breastfeeding can help protect your baby from various illnesses, such as ear infections, respiratory infections, and gastrointestinal problems.
- **Cognitive Benefits:** Studies suggest breastfed babies may have higher IQs and better cognitive development.
- **Emotional Benefits:** Breastfeeding can strengthen the bond between mother and child.

Benefits of Formula Feeding

- **Flexibility:** Formula feeding allows for more flexibility in feeding schedules and can be shared by multiple caregivers.
- **Nutritional Adequacy:** Modern formulas are carefully formulated to provide essential nutrients for a baby's growth and development.
- **Reduced Stress:** Formula feeding can alleviate the stress associated with breastfeeding challenges, such as low milk supply or painful latching.

Ultimately, the most important factor is to provide your baby with love, care, and nutritious food. Whether you choose to breastfeed or formula-feed, it's crucial to consult with your paediatrician to ensure your baby's optimal health and well-being.

When to Introduce Solid Foods

You should start introducing solid foods to your baby around 6 months of age. Look for these signs of readiness:

- **Strong head and neck control:** Your baby can steady their head.
- **Interest in food:** They watch you eat and may open their mouth when food is near.
- **Loss of the tongue-thrust reflex:** They no longer automatically push food out with their tongue.

Important Note: It's crucial to consult with your paediatrician before introducing solid foods, especially if your baby has any specific health concerns.

Safe Foods to Introduce

When starting solids, it is best to introduce one new food at a time, waiting a few days between each new food to monitor for allergic reactions. Here are some safe food options to consider:

First Foods

- **Iron-fortified infant cereal:** Rice cereal is a common first food, but consider other options like barley or oat cereal.
- **Pureed fruits:** Applesauce, bananas, pears, and avocados are good choices.
- **Pureed vegetables:** Sweet potatoes, carrots, and peas are gentle on a baby's digestive system.

Later Foods

As your baby grows, you can gradually introduce more textured foods and a wider variety of flavours:

- **Mashed or soft-cooked vegetables:** Broccoli, cauliflower, and green beans.
- **Mashed or soft-cooked fruits:** Berries, peaches, and plums.
- **Meat and poultry:** Well-cooked and ground or shredded.
- **Eggs:** Scrambled or hard-boiled.
- **Yogurt:** Plain, unsweetened yogurt.
- **Cheese:** Soft, mild cheeses like cottage cheese or cream cheese.

Remember

- **Avoid honey and cow's milk:** These can increase the risk of infant botulism.
- **Introduce allergenic foods gradually:** Foods like eggs, nuts, and shellfish can be introduced after 6 months.
- **Avoid added sugars and salts:** These can harm a baby's developing kidneys.
- **Offer plenty of water:** As your baby starts eating solids, ensure they stay hydrated.

Always consult your paediatrician for personalised advice and to address any specific concerns you may have.

Identifying and Managing Food Allergies in Your Baby

You may be asking: how can I identify and manage food allergies in my baby?

Identifying Food Allergies

- **Watch for Symptoms**
    - Skin reactions: Hives, eczema, or swelling of the lips, tongue, or throat.
    - Digestive issues: Diarrhoea, vomiting, or abdominal pain.
    - Respiratory symptoms: Wheezing, coughing, or difficulty breathing.
- **Keep a Food Diary**
    - Track your baby's diet and any symptoms arising after eating specific foods.

Always consult your paediatrician, who can provide guidance and recommend allergy testing if necessary.

Managing Food Allergies

Once a food allergy is identified, it's crucial to avoid that food and any products containing it strictly.

- **Read Labels Carefully:** Always check food labels for allergens, even in seemingly unrelated products.
- **Emergency Preparedness:** Keep an epinephrine auto-injector (EpiPen) on hand if your child has a severe allergy.
- **Inform Caregivers:** Ensure that all caregivers, including daycare providers and teachers, know your child's allergies and how to respond to an allergic reaction.
- **Allergy-Friendly Meals:** Prepare meals at home or choose allergen-free options when eating out.
- **Avoid Cross-Contamination:** Use separate utensils and cutting boards for allergenic foods.

- **Educate Your Child:** Teach your child about their allergies and how to avoid triggers.

Remember

- **Early introduction of allergenic foods:** In many cases, introducing allergenic foods early in infancy can actually reduce the risk of developing allergies. Consult with your paediatrician for personalised advice.
- **Consult with a Registered Dietitian:** A registered dietitian can help you create a balanced and nutritious diet for your child, even with food allergies.

If your child experiences a severe allergic reaction, seek immediate medical attention.

Sleep Regressions: Navigating the Bumpy Nights

What are sleep regressions?

Sleep regressions are periods where your baby's sleep patterns become disrupted. They often occur around developmental milestones, such as rolling over, crawling, or sitting up. During these periods, your baby may wake up more frequently, have trouble falling asleep, or sleep for shorter periods.

How to Cope with Sleep Regressions

1. **Stay Consistent:** Maintain a consistent sleep routine, including bedtime, bath time, and a quiet wind-down period.
2. **Create a Calm Sleep Environment:** Ensure the room is dark, quiet, and at a comfortable temperature.
3. **Offer Comfort:** Provide gentle comfort, such as patting or shushing, but avoid picking your baby up unless necessary.
4. **Avoid Overtiredness:** Be mindful of your baby's wake windows and avoid overstimulation close to bedtime.
5. **Trust the Process:** Remember that sleep regressions are temporary, and your baby will eventually return to regular sleep patterns.
6. **Seek Professional Help:** Consult a paediatrician or a sleep consultant for personalised advice if you're struggling to cope.

Nighttime Awakenings: Understanding the Causes

Nighttime awakenings can be frustrating for both parents and babies. Here are some common reasons why your baby may be waking up at night:

- **Hunger:** Ensure your baby gets enough milk during the day and at night.
- **Teething:** Teething can cause discomfort and disrupt sleep.
- **Illness:** If your baby is sick, they may wake up more often.
- **Developmental Leaps:** As your baby grows and learns new skills, they may experience sleep disturbances.
- **Overtiredness:** Too much daytime stimulation can lead to nighttime awakenings.

Tips for Reducing Nighttime Awakenings

- **Establish a Bedtime Routine:** A consistent routine can signal to your baby that it's time to sleep.
- **Create a Calm Sleep Environment:** A dark, quiet, and cool room can promote better sleep.
- **Offer Comfort:** Provide gentle comfort, such as patting or shushing, but avoid picking your baby up unless necessary.
- **Consider Sleep Training:** Consult with a paediatrician or sleep consultant for guidance on gentle sleep training methods.

Swaddling: A Safe and Effective Sleep Aid

Swaddling can be a helpful tool to promote sleep, especially for newborns. However, it is important to swaddle your baby safely:

- **Use a Swaddle Blanket:** A swaddle blanket explicitly designed for babies is the safest option.
- **Swaddle Loosely:** The swaddle should be loose enough for your baby to move their hips and legs.
- **Stop Swaddling When Necessary:** As your baby starts to roll over, you should stop swaddling to prevent accidents.

Understanding the reasons behind sleep disturbances and implementing effective strategies can help your baby sleep better and improve your family's overall well-being.

Immunisations: A Shield Against Disease

Immunisations are one of the most effective ways to protect your child from serious, sometimes life-threatening diseases. The recommended immunisation schedule varies slightly by country but generally includes vaccines for:

- **Diphtheria, tetanus, and pertussis (DTaP)**
- **Polio**
- **Measles, mumps, and rubella (MMR)**
- **Haemophilus influenza type b (Hib)**
- **Varicella (chickenpox)**
- **Pneumococcal disease**
- **Rotavirus**

Safety of Immunisations: Immunisations have been extensively studied and proven safe and effective. While some children may experience mild side effects like soreness at the injection site or a low-grade fever, serious side effects are rare.

Common Childhood Illnesses and Prevention

- **Respiratory Syncytial Virus (RSV):** A common respiratory virus that can cause cold-like symptoms or more severe lung infections. Prevention includes handwashing, avoiding sick people, and, in some cases, medication.
- **Influenza (Flu):** A contagious respiratory illness. Annual flu shots are recommended to protect your child.
- **Common Cold:** Caused by various viruses. Prevention includes handwashing, avoiding sick people, and ensuring adequate rest and hydration.

First Aid Skills for Baby Safety

Here are some essential first-aid skills to learn:

- **CPR and First Aid:** Taking a certified infant and child CPR and first aid course is crucial.
- **Choking:** Learn the Heimlich manoeuvre for infants.
- **Burns:** Treat burns with cool water and avoid applying ointments or butter.
- **Cuts and Scrapes:** Clean the wound with mild soap and water, apply gentle pressure to stop bleeding, and cover with a clean bandage.
- **Fever:** Monitor your baby's temperature and administer fever reducers as your paediatrician directs.
- **Poisoning:** Call your local poison control centre immediately.

By understanding these topics, you can proactively protect your child's health and well-being. Always consult with your paediatrician for personalised advice and guidance.

Teething: Soothing Your Baby's Discomfort

Teething can be a challenging time for both baby and parent. Here are some tips to soothe your baby:

- **Teething Rings:** Offer chilled teething rings to help soothe sore gums.
- **Gentle Massage:** Gently massage your baby's gums with a clean finger.
- **Cold Foods:** Offer cold foods like chilled fruits or a cold spoon.
- **Over-the-counter Pain Relief:** Consult your paediatrician about using over-the-counter pain relievers, such as acetaminophen or ibuprofen.
- **Comfort:** Offer extra cuddles, rocking, or singing to comfort your baby.

Separation Anxiety: Helping Your Baby Cope

Separation anxiety is a normal developmental stage that many babies go through. Here are some strategies to help your baby cope:

- **Gradual Separations:** Start with short separations and gradually increase the duration.
- **Consistent Routines:** Stick to a consistent routine to provide a sense of security.
- **Positive Departures:** Say goodbye cheerfully and avoid prolonged goodbyes.

- **Comfort Objects:** Provide a comfort object, like a favourite toy or blanket.
- **Trustworthy Caregivers:** Ensure your baby is with trusted caregivers who can provide comfort.

Tantrums: Handling Them Calmly and Effectively

Tantrums are a normal part of child development. Here are some tips to handle them effectively:

- **Stay Calm:** Your calm demeanour can help de-escalate the situation.
- **Avoid Reacting:** Avoid reacting to the tantrum with anger or frustration.
- **Set Limits:** Clearly state expectations and enforce limits calmly.
- **Offer Choices:** Give your child choices to help them feel in control.
- **Distraction Techniques:** Redirect your child's attention to a different activity.
- **Time-Outs:** A brief time-out can help older children calm down.
- **Positive Reinforcement:** Reward positive behaviour to encourage it.

Remember, it is important to be patient and understanding. Seek guidance from your paediatrician if you have concerns about your child's behaviour or development

Stimulating Activities for Your Baby

Stimulating activities can help your baby's brain develop and learn new skills. Here are some ideas:

- **Tummy Time:** Place your baby on their tummy for short periods to strengthen their neck and back muscles.
- **Sensory Play:** Provide opportunities for sensory experiences, such as touching different textures, playing with water, and listening to music.
- **Reading:** Read books to your baby to stimulate language development and imagination.
- **Singing and Talking:** Sing and talk to your baby to encourage language development.
- **Playtime:** Engage in interactive play, such as peek-a-boo and hide-and-seek.
- **Outdoor Activities:** Spend time outdoors to explore nature and get fresh air.

Remember, every baby develops at their own pace. If you have any concerns about your baby's development, consult with your paediatrician.

Vision and Hearing Problems: Early Detection is Key

Regular check-ups with your paediatrician are crucial for early detection of potential vision or hearing problems.

Here are some signs that may indicate a vision or hearing issue:

- **Vision:**
  - Crossing or turning eyes
  - Blinking excessively

- o Avoiding eye contact
- o Difficulty tracking objects
- o Squinting or holding objects close to the face
- **Hearing:**
  - o Lack of response to sounds
  - o Difficulty following verbal commands
  - o Frequent ear infections
  - o Turning head to one side to hear

Motor Delays: Seeking Professional Advice

Consult your paediatrician if you notice delays in your baby's motor development, such as difficulty rolling over, sitting up, crawling, or walking. Early intervention can help address any underlying issues and promote optimal development.

Feeding Issues: Addressing Challenges

Feeding issues can be frustrating for both parents and babies. Consult your paediatrician if you notice excessive fussiness, difficulty swallowing, or other feeding problems. They can help identify the underlying cause and recommend appropriate strategies.

Sleep Problems: Getting Quality Rest

Sleep problems can affect your baby's overall well-being and development. If your baby has difficulty falling asleep, waking up frequently, or experiencing other sleep disturbances, **consult your paediatrician**. They can advise on establishing healthy sleep habits and address any underlying issues.

Remember, early intervention is key to addressing developmental concerns. Don't hesitate to seek professional advice if you have questions or concerns about your baby's development.

Balancing Work and Family Life

Balancing work and family life can be challenging but possible with effective planning and support. Here are some tips:

- **Prioritise:** Identify what is most important and focus on those tasks.
- **Time Management:** Use time management techniques like blocking and to-do lists.
- **Delegate:** Don't be afraid to delegate tasks to others, whether your partner, family members, or hired help.
- **Set Boundaries:** Establish clear boundaries between work and family time.
- **Self-Care:** Make time for yourself to recharge and reduce stress.

Self-Care for Busy Parents

Taking care of yourself is essential for being a good parent. Here are some self-care tips:

- **Physical Self-Care:** Prioritise sleep, eat healthy, and exercise regularly.
- **Mental Self-Care:** Practice mindfulness techniques like meditation or yoga.
- **Emotional Self-Care:** Connect with loved ones, pursue hobbies, and seek support when needed.

Maintaining a Strong Relationship

A strong relationship with your partner is crucial for your and your child's well-being. Here are some tips:

- **Communicate Openly:** Talk about your feelings, needs, and expectations.
- **Date Nights:** Schedule regular date nights to reconnect.
- **Share Responsibilities:** Divide household chores and childcare duties fairly.
- **Support Each Other:** Be each other's support system, especially during challenging times.
- **Seek Help:** Consider couples therapy or counselling if you're struggling.

Remember, asking for help and setting realistic expectations is okay. You can balance work, family, and relationships by prioritising self-care, effective communication, and a strong support system.

Mindful Munches: Addressing Common Concerns and Questions

Remember that the first year of your child's life is filled with joy and wonder, but it can also be a time of uncertainty and questions. It's natural to have concerns about feeding, sleep, development, and behaviour. By seeking information, connecting with other parents, and consulting with healthcare professionals, you can find the answers and support you need to navigate this critical stage of your child's life. Remember, every child is unique, and there is no one-size-fits-all approach to parenting. Trust your instincts, seek guidance when needed, and enjoy the precious moments with your little one.

Chapter 8: Looking Forward

Preparing for Toddlerhood

- **Understanding the Challenges:** Be prepared for the challenges of toddlerhood, such as tantrums, defiance, and increased independence.
- **Providing Positive Discipline:** Learn effective discipline strategies that promote positive behaviour and foster a strong parent-child relationship.
- **Encouraging Exploration:** Provide a safe and stimulating environment for your toddler to explore and learn.

Continued Development

- **Physical Development:** Expect your toddler to continue to grow and develop physically, including gaining weight, increasing height, and refining motor skills.
- **Cognitive Development:** Support your toddler's cognitive development by providing opportunities for learning and problem-solving.
- **Language Development:** Encourage your toddler's language development by reading, talking, and singing with them.
- **Social and Emotional Development:** Help your toddler develop social skills, manage emotions, and build relationships with others.

Building a Strong Foundation

- **The Importance of Early Childhood Experiences:** Understand the crucial role of early childhood experiences in shaping a child's development.
- **Nurturing Relationships:** Foster strong and loving relationships with your child to provide a solid foundation for their emotional well-being.
- **Supporting Learning and Growth:** Continue to provide opportunities for learning and growth throughout your child's early years.
- **Preparing for Preschool or Kindergarten:** If applicable, start preparing your child for preschool or kindergarten by helping them develop essential skills and social interactions.

Remember, every child is unique, and their development will vary. By providing a loving, supportive, and stimulating environment, you can help your child reach their full potential.

Mindful Munches: A Foundation for a Lifetime

The first year of your baby's life is precious and transformative. This period of your child's life is a whirlwind of growth and development, laying the groundwork for their future. During this crucial period, nurturing their physical, emotional, and cognitive needs is paramount. By providing a stimulating environment, responding to their cues, and engaging in interactive play, you're helping them develop the skills necessary for a smooth transition into toddlerhood. A strong foundation in these early years will set the stage for your child's future development and create a lifelong bond between you.

I am so proud of you and your precious angel!

 Look how far you have come!

Chapter 9: A Tapestry of Parenthood

Mindful Munches: You Are Never Alone

Parent 1: The Nursing Mother

As a nurse, Chantelle was no stranger to demanding schedules and sleepless nights. But nothing could have prepared her for the whirlwind of emotions and challenges of becoming a mother of two. Juggling her newborn and toddler's demands, Chantelle found herself stretched thin yet filled with an overwhelming sense of love and purpose. She learned to prioritise self-care, rely on her support system, and embrace the chaos of motherhood.

Parent 2: The Teacher's Journey

After a challenging C-section delivery, Pearlyn returned home to a newborn and a toddler, feeling both overwhelmed and exhilarated. As a teacher, she was used to structure and routine, but motherhood brought a new level of unpredictability. She learned to adapt her teaching skills to her new role as a mother, finding creative ways to engage her toddler while caring for her newborn.

Parent 3: The College Student's Struggle

Debbia's world was turned upside down when her premature baby was born, and her relationship ended in divorce. As a college student, she faced immense challenges juggling her studies, caring for her newborn, healing from a C-Section, and navigating the emotional turmoil of a breakup. Despite the hardships, Debbia found strength and resilience, leaning on her support system and prioritising her and her baby's well-being.

Parent 4: A Father's Unwavering Resolve

Javin's world changed when his partner left, leaving him to raise their children alone. Fear and uncertainty gnawed at him, but he knew he had to be strong for his children. With unwavering determination, he embarked on this unfamiliar journey. Javin learned to wash, soothe his crying children, and feed his children with a tenderness that surprised even himself. He juggled parenthood with work responsibilities, finding solace in his love for his children. Though there were moments of doubt and exhaustion, Javin's courage and tenacity never wavered. He faced each challenge with resilience, proving that a single father could provide his children with a loving and nurturing home.

Parent 5 The Mother of a Child with Dwarfism

Raising a child with dwarfism presented unique challenges for Rosie. She faced questions, stereotypes, and the need to advocate for her child's needs. Through it all, Rosie found a community of supportive parents and learned to embrace her child's individuality and strengths.

Parent 6: The Single Mother's Resilience

Tina's world was shattered when her partner passed away shortly after she gave birth. As a single mother, she faced immense grief and uncertainty. Yet, she found the strength to persevere, leaning on her family and friends for support. She learned to be self-sufficient and create a loving and stable environment for her children.

Parent 7: The Blessed Mother

With a strong family support system, Maureen navigated the challenges of motherhood with grace and ease. She cherished quality time with her children, knowing she was blessed with a loving and supportive family.

Parent 8: The Rejected Mother

Rejected by her lover and his family after giving birth to a baby boy, Denise felt isolated and alone. She faced judgment and discrimination, but she refused to give up on her child. With unwavering determination, Denise built a support network of other mothers and found the strength to raise her son with love and resilience.

Parent 9: The High School Grandaunt

Donna's life took an unexpected turn when she became pregnant shortly after graduating high school. As a single mother facing the challenges of raising a newborn, she demonstrated remarkable resilience and courage. The unexpected c-section, though daunting, did not deter her from her unwavering commitment to her child. With steadfast determination, she navigated the complexities of motherhood, balancing her newfound responsibilities with her aspirations for the future. Her journey was a testament to the strength and resilience of young mothers, proving that even in the face of adversity, love and hope can prevail.

Parent 10: A Mother's Unwavering Love

Candy's resilience was a testament to the strength of the human spirit. Despite the overwhelming grief that followed Shanoya's loss, she refused to let despair consume her. She found solace in the memories of her child, cherishing the short time they had together. With each passing day, she discovered a newfound strength and determination to live on for Shanoya's sake. Her journey was a poignant reminder that hope and resilience can prevail even in the darkest times.

Parent 11: A School Counsellor's Unwavering Resilience

Pauline's world was turned upside down when her marriage ended in divorce, leaving her as a single mother eagerly anticipating the arrival of her child. After a long-awaited pregnancy, she underwent a caesarean section, only to face another major surgery nine months later. Despite the challenges, Pauline found unwavering support from her school family and friends, who rallied around her during this difficult time. Her extended labour, a result of her initial naivety, further tested her resilience. However, Pauline's determination and adaptability allowed her to navigate the complexities of work-life balance and motherhood with grace and strength.

Mindful Munches: Stories of Strength, Resilience, and Love

The stories told in this book offer a glimpse into the diverse experiences of parenthood, highlighting the challenges, triumphs, and unwavering love that parents possess. Each parent faced unique obstacles, but they all found strength, resilience, and unwavering love for their children. Their experiences taught them valuable lessons about self-care, support, and the enduring bond between parent and child.

Regardless of your struggles, remember that you are never alone. Seek support from your loved ones, join parenting groups, or consult with professionals. Remember, your love for your child is a powerful force that can help you overcome any challenge.

Chapter 10: Seeking Expert Advice

When to Consult a Paediatrician or Child Development Specialist

It's essential to seek professional advice from paediatricians and child development specialists for various reasons, including:

- **Developmental Concerns:** If you have concerns about your child's development, such as delayed milestones or unusual behaviours, consulting with a professional can provide reassurance and guidance.
- **Medical Issues:** Paediatricians can diagnose and treat medical conditions affecting your child's development.
- **Behavioural Challenges:** If you're facing difficulties with your child's behaviour, such as tantrums, aggression, or social withdrawal, a child development specialist can offer strategies and support.
- **Learning Difficulties:** If you suspect your child may have learning difficulties, a child development specialist can assess their skills and recommend appropriate interventions.
- **Special Needs:** If your child has special needs, such as autism or developmental delays, a team of professionals can provide comprehensive support and guidance.

How to Find a Paediatrician or a Child Development Specialist

- **Ask for Recommendations:** Ask your friends, family, or healthcare provider.
- **Research Online:** Look for paediatricians and child development specialists in your area using online directories.

- **Contact Your Insurance Provider:** Your insurance provider may have a list of recommended professionals.
- **Check with Local Hospitals or Clinics:** Hospitals and clinics often have paediatric departments and child development centres.

What to Expect When Consulting a Professional

When you consult with a paediatrician or child development specialist, be prepared to discuss your child's development, any concerns you have, and your family's history. The professional will likely conduct a thorough evaluation to assess your child's skills and identify any areas of concern.

The professional may provide recommendations for further assessment, interventions, or support services based on the evaluation. They may also offer guidance on how to support your child's development at home.

Remember, seeking professional advice is a proactive step to ensure your child's well-being and support their optimal development.

Prioritise Self-Care

For your health and well-being, parents need to prioritise self-care. This includes:

- **Physical Health:** Eating a balanced diet, exercising regularly, and ensuring adequate sleep.
- **Mental Health:** Taking time for relaxation, stress management, and seeking support when needed.

- **Emotional Well-being:** Nurturing positive relationships, practising mindfulness, and finding activities that bring joy and fulfilment.
- **Self-Care Activities:** Incorporating self-care activities into your routine, such as bathing, reading, or spending time in nature.

Parents can better support their children and create a positive family environment by caring for themselves.

Mindful Munches: The Importance of Professional Help for New Parents, Including Postnatal Depression

Navigating the early stages of parenthood can be overwhelming, especially for parents who are experiencing postnatal depression. Seeking professional help from paediatricians, lactation consultants, or child development specialists can provide invaluable guidance and support. These professionals can offer expert advice on infant care, nutrition, sleep, and developmental milestones. They can also help identify and address any potential concerns or challenges you may be facing, including symptoms of postnatal depression.

Postnatal depression is a serious condition that affects many new mothers and fathers. It can lead to feelings of sadness, anxiety, and hopelessness. If you are experiencing any of these symptoms, it is important to seek help. A professional can provide a diagnosis, recommend appropriate treatment options, and offer emotional support. By seeking professional help, you can gain valuable insights, develop effective coping strategies, and build a strong foundation for your child's future while also taking care of your mental health.

Mindful Munches

Milestones and Moments presents a tapestry of parenthood and offers a simple guide for parents, providing valuable information, support, and inspiration. Here are the key messages:

The Diverse Experiences of Parenthood

- **Overcoming Challenges:** Parents face many challenges, including financial difficulties, health issues, relationship problems, and societal pressures.
- **Finding Strength and Resilience:** Despite these challenges, parents demonstrate remarkable strength, resilience, and unwavering love for their children.
- **Building a Support Network:** A strong support system is crucial for navigating the challenges of parenthood.

The Importance of Self-Care

- **Prioritising Self-Care:** Taking care of oneself is essential for physical and mental well-being.
- **Finding Balance:** Balancing the demands of parenthood with personal needs is crucial for long-term health and happiness.
- **Seeking Support:** Don't hesitate to seek support from friends, family, or professionals when needed.

The Power of Love and Connection

- **Unconditional Love:** The love between a parent and child is a powerful and enduring bond.
- **Building Relationships:** Nurturing strong relationships with your child and others can provide emotional support and enrichment.
- **Creating Lasting Memories:** Cherish the precious moments and create lasting memories with your child.

The Importance of Early Childhood Development

- **Understanding Milestones:** Familiarize yourself with your child's developmental milestones and provide appropriate support.
- **Creating a Stimulating Environment:** Foster your child's development by providing a safe and stimulating environment.
- **Seeking Professional Advice:** Consult with paediatricians and child development specialists for guidance and support.

Building a Strong Foundation for the Future

- **Early Childhood Experiences:** The early years of childhood are crucial for a child's development and lifelong well-being.

- **Nurturing Relationships:** Building strong and loving relationships with your child can impact their emotional health.
- **Supporting Learning and Growth:** Providing opportunities for learning and growth can help your child reach their full potential.

By understanding these key messages, parents can better navigate the challenges and joys of parenthood, building a solid foundation for their children's future.

Thank you for taking me on this wonderful journey with you!

Chapter 11: Choosing a Nanny/Caregiver - Enriching Your Baby's First Year

Choosing a caregiver or nanny for your baby's first year is a big decision. Here are some tips that might help you find the right person:

- **Start your search early:** Begin your search well in advance to allow enough time for interviews and background checks. This is very important if you want to return to work soon after giving birth.
- **Ask for recommendations:** Reach out to friends, family, and other parents for recommendations.
- **Check references:** Contact previous employers and families to learn more about the caregiver's experience and skills.
- **Interview potential caregivers:** Ask about their experience, childcare philosophy, and availability.
- **Observe their interactions with your baby:** Pay attention to how the caregiver interacts with your baby and how your baby responds to them.
- **Trust your instincts:** Don't hesitate to move on to another candidate if something feels off.

Some Key Qualities to Look for in a Nanny/ Caregiver:

Essential Qualities:

- **Love for Children:** A genuine passion for working with children is crucial.
- **Reliability and Punctuality:** A nanny should be dependable and arrive on time.

- **Patience and Calmness:** The ability to handle stressful situations and tantrums with patience.
- **Good Communication Skills:** Clear and open communication with parents and children.
- **Strong Work Ethic:** A willingness to take initiative and complete tasks efficiently.
- **First Aid and CPR Certified:** Essential for handling emergencies.
- **Background Check:** A thorough background check to ensure safety.
- **Training:** Child safeguarding training

Additional Qualities:

- **Experience:** Previous experience working with children, especially infants and toddlers.
- **Education:** Childcare training or early childhood education background.
- **Creativity:** Ability to develop engaging activities and games for children.
- **Flexibility:** Adaptability to changing schedules and routines.
- **Positive Attitude:** A cheerful and optimistic demeanour.
- **Trustworthiness:** Honesty and integrity.

During the Interview Process, Consider Asking:

- Their childcare philosophy and approach to discipline.
- Their experience with infants and toddlers.
- How they handle emergencies and accidents.
- Their availability and willingness to work flexible hours.
- Their expectations for compensation and benefits.

Remember, finding the right nanny is a personal decision. Trust your instincts and choose someone with whom you feel comfortable leaving your child. Also, the most important thing is to find a caregiver who you trust and who will provide your baby with love, care, and attention.

Chapter 12: Choosing an Early Childhood Setting for Your Infant

Quality of Care:

- **Licensing and Accreditation:** Ensure the facility is licensed and accredited by relevant authorities. This indicates adherence to specific standards of care.
- **Staff Qualifications:** Look for caregivers with training and experience in early childhood education.
- **Staff-to-Child Ratio:** A lower staff-to-child ratio ensures more individualised attention for your infant.
- **Curriculum:** A well-structured curriculum that promotes cognitive, social, emotional, and physical development.

Safety:

- **Safe Environment:** The facility should be clean, well-maintained, and free from hazards.
- **Security Measures:** Secure entry points, childproofing, and emergency procedures in place.
- **Health and Hygiene:** Strict adherence to health and hygiene protocols to minimise the spread of illness.
- **Safeguarding Arrangements:** All staff trained in Child Safeguarding and Cardiopulmonary Resuscitation. (CPR)

Child's Needs:

- **Individualised Attention:** The ability to cater to your child's needs and temperament.

- **Nurturing Environment:** A warm, loving, and supportive atmosphere.
- **Opportunities for Social Interaction:** Encouragement of social interaction with other children.
- **Healthy Meals and Snacks:** Nutritious meals and snacks provided.

Your Comfort and Peace of Mind:

- **Communication:** Regular communication with caregivers about your child's day.
- **Flexibility:** Accommodating your family's schedule and needs.
- **Trust and Rapport:** A strong relationship with the caregivers.
- **Cost:** Consider the cost of care and any additional fees.

Additional Tips:

- **Visit the Facility:** Take a tour of the facility to get a firsthand look at the environment and see it firsthand.
- **Talk to Other Parents:** Seek recommendations from other parents and get feedback on their experiences.
- **Trust Your Instincts:** Don't hesitate to look elsewhere if something doesn't feel right.

By carefully considering these factors, you can choose an early childhood setting that will provide your infant a safe, nurturing, and stimulating environment.

Chapter 13: Nanny/Caregiver versus Early Childhood Settings: A Comparative Analysis

Nanny/Caregiver

Advantages:

- **Personalised Attention:** Nannies can provide one-on-one care, tailoring activities to your child's needs and interests.
- **Consistent Care:** Nannies offer consistent care in a familiar home environment, reducing stress for the child.
- **Flexible Schedule:** Nannies can often accommodate flexible schedules to fit your family's needs.
- **Strong Bond:** Nannies can develop deep bonds with children, providing emotional support and stability.

Disadvantages:

- **Socialisation:** Children may have limited social interaction with other children, potentially affecting social skills development.
- **Cost:** Hiring a nanny can be more expensive than enrolling a child in a childcare centre.
- **Reliability:** Nannies may be more prone to illness or personal emergencies, leading to potential disruptions in childcare.
- **Isolation:** Nannies may feel isolated, especially if they work long hours without adult interaction.

Early Childhood Settings

Advantages:

- **Socialisation:** Children can interact with peers, learning valuable social skills like sharing, cooperation, and conflict resolution.
- **Structured Learning:** Early childhood settings often provide structured learning activities, such as art, music, and literacy, to promote cognitive development.
- **Professional Care:** Childcare providers are often trained in early childhood education and development.
- **Backup Care:** Many childcare centres offer backup care options for unexpected situations.

Disadvantages:

- **Less Personalized Attention:** Children may receive less individualised attention than one-on-one care with a nanny.
- **Exposure to Illness:** Children in group settings are more likely to be exposed to illnesses.
- **Less Flexibility:** Childcare centres typically have fixed hours of operation.
- **Transition Period:** Children may need time to adjust to a new environment and routine.

Ultimately, the best choice for your family will depend on your child's individual needs, your family's lifestyle, and your budget. Consider the pros and cons of each option carefully to make an informed decision.

Some Online Communities for Parents

There are numerous online communities where parents can connect with others, share experiences, and seek support. Here are a few popular options:

General Parenting Forums

- **BabyCenter:** https://www.babycenter.com/
- **Parents.com:** https://www.parents.com/
- **The Bump:** https://www.thebump.com/
- **Pearls Petals and Pulse:** https://pearlspetalsandpulse.com/

Parenting Forums Focused on Specific Topics

- **Breastfeeding Support:** La Leche League International (LLL) https://llli.org/
- **Autism Spectrum Disorder:** Autism Speaks https://www.autismspeaks.org/
- **Special Needs Parenting:** The Arc https://thearc.org/
- **Single Parenting:** Single Mothers by Choice https://www.singlemothersbychoice.org/

Social Media Platforms

- **Facebook Groups:** There are countless Facebook groups dedicated to parenting, from general parenting to specific topics like breastfeeding, toddlerhood, or parenting with disabilities.
- **Reddit:** Reddit has numerous parenting subreddits where you can find discussions, advice, and support.

Local Parenting Groups

- **Check with Your Local Library or Community Centre:** These organisations often host parenting groups or can connect you with local resources.
- **Online Directories:** Search online for local parenting groups in your area.

When choosing an online community, consider the following factors

- **Topic Relevance:** Choose a community that focuses on topics relevant to your parenting needs.
- **Support and Positivity:** Look for communities that offer supportive and positive interactions.
- **Privacy:** Be mindful of privacy settings and avoid sharing personal information that you don't want to be public.

By joining an online community, you can connect with other parents, share experiences, seek advice, and find support in your parenting journey.

Unlocking Extra Support: Join Our Milestones and Mochas Community!

Thank you for choosing "Milestones and Moments" as your guide to navigating your baby's first year! We're thrilled you're on this incredible journey with us.

We understand that parenthood comes with countless questions and moments where you might crave support. That's why we're excited to introduce you to **Milestones & Mochas**, a vibrant online community designed for parents just like you!

What to expect at Milestones & Mochas

- **Connect with other parents**: Share experiences, ask questions, and offer support in a safe and encouraging environment.

- **Expert insights**: Gain valuable tips and advice from parenting professionals and early childhood development specialists.
- **Milestone celebrations**: Celebrate your baby's achievements alongside other parents as your little one grows and learns.

Grab an "I Love Coffee Shirt" and Join Milestones and Mochas today!

Simply visit https://pearlspetalsandpulse.com/ for information on Milestones and Mochas. Do not hesitate to contact us at pearlspetalsandpulse@gmail.com if you have any questions.

Mindful Munches

Remember that caffeine can pass through breast milk, so it is imperative to be mindful of your intake while breastfeeding. While moderate amounts are generally safe, excessive caffeine consumption can affect your baby's sleep patterns and behaviour. Some babies are more sensitive to caffeine than others.

Here are some tips for managing caffeine intake while breastfeeding:

- **Limit intake:** Aim for no more than 200-300 milligrams of caffeine daily. This is equivalent to about 1-2 cups of coffee.
- **Time your caffeine intake:** Try to consume caffeine after a feeding session to minimise its impact on your baby.
- **Monitor your baby's response:**

If you notice your baby becoming fussy, irritable, or having trouble sleeping, consider reducing caffeine intake.

- **Consider decaf options:** Decaffeinated coffee or tea can be a good alternative if you crave the flavour without the caffeine.

If you have concerns about caffeine consumption and breastfeeding, it's always best to consult your healthcare provider or a lactation consultant. They can provide personalised advice based on your specific situation.

We look forward to welcoming you to Milestones and Mochas!

Warmly,

The Pearl's Brain Bakery Team

The "Focus and Play" Travel Kit To Aid Social And Physical Development

The resources for the "Focus and Play" travel kit were handpicked from various sources and placed in an easy portable kit. This kit was designed to provide children with engaging and stimulating activities to help them focus, stay calm, and reduce screen time during travel or waiting periods. The kit includes a variety of sensory toys, such as fidget spinners, stress balls, and texture cards, to keep little hands busy and minds occupied. These toys are fun and help develop fine motor skills and sensory processing.

Additionally, the kit includes quiet activities like colouring books, stickers, and puzzles to encourage creativity and problem-solving. By providing these alternative forms of entertainment, the "Focus and Play" travel kit helps to promote a more peaceful and enjoyable travel experience for both children and parents.

Warmly,

The Pearl's Brain Bakery Team

Books from the Author

Grit & Grace: Guiding Young Children's Behaviour

Whispers of Wonder: A Parenthood Journal for Guiding Tiny Hearts

Moving From Theory to Practice: A Reflective Journal for Teachers

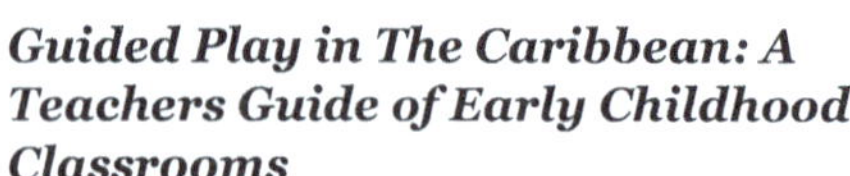

Guided Play in The Caribbean: A Teachers Guide of Early Childhood Classrooms

New Mom, New Life! A Guide to Navigating Motherhood with Confidence, Care and Grace